GALAXY OF SUPERSTARS

98°	Hanson
Aerosmith	Jennifer Love Hewitt
Ben Affleck	Faith Hill
Jennifer Aniston	Lauryn Hill
Backstreet Boys	Heath Ledger
Drew Barrymore	Jennifer Lopez
Beck	Ricky Martin
Brandy	Ewan McGregor
Garth Brooks	Mike Myers
Mariah Carey	'N Sync
Matt Damon	Gwyneth Paltrow
Dave Matthews Band	LeAnn Rimes
Destiny's Child	Adam Sandler
Cameron Diaz	Will Smith
Leonardo DiCaprio	Britney Spears
Céline Dion	Spice Girls
Dixie Chicks	Ben Stiller
Sarah Michelle Gellar	Jonathan Taylor Thomas
Tom Hanks	Venus Williams

CHELSEA HOUSE PUBLISHERS

GALAXY OF SUPERSTARS

Dave Matthews Band

Erik Anjou

CHELSEA HOUSE PUBLISHERS
Philadelphia

Frontis: Dave Matthews' road to success with the Dave Matthews Band has been a long and arduous one, but today he and his bandmates continue to entertain and inspire with their integrity, musicianship and innovation.

CHELSEA HOUSE PUBLISHERS
Editor in Chief: Sally Cheney
Director of Production: Kim Shinners
Creative Manager: Takeshi Takahashi
Manufacturing Manager: Diann Grasse

Staff for DAVE MATTHEWS BAND
Associate Editor: Ben Kim
Picture Researcher: Jane Sanders
Production Assistant: Jaimie Winkler
Series Designer: Takeshi Takahashi
Cover Designer: Terry Mallon
Layout: 21st Century Publishing and Communications, Inc.

The Chelsea House World Wide Web address is
http://www.chelseahouse.com

First Printing

1 3 5 7 9 8 6 4 2

Library of Congress Cataloging-in-Publication Data

Anjou, Erik.
  Dave Matthews Band / by Erik Anjou.
    p. cm. — (Galaxy of superstars)
Summary: An account of the formation of the Dave Matthews Band and
its rise to become one of the top groups in the world of rock music.
Includes bibliographical references (p.   ) and index.
  ISBN 0-7910-6765-3
  1. Dave Matthews Band—Juvenile literature. 2. Matthews, Dave,
1967– —Juvenile literature. 3. Rock musicians—United States—
Biography—Juvenile literature. [1. Dave Mathews Band. 2. Matthews,
Dave, 1967– 3. Musicians. 4. Rock music.] I. Title. II. Series.
ML3930.D326 A55 2002
781.66'092'2—dc21
                                              2002000846

Contents

1

THE WATCHER

It was June 1999. David John Matthews was 32 years old and seriously depressed. He was hunkered down in Charlottesville, Virginia with the rest of the Dave Matthews Band in a rented house whose basement the band had converted into a recording studio. The core of the five-member Dave Matthews Band (DMB) consists of Dave, Carter Beauford (vocals and drums), Boyd Tinsley (violin), Leroi Moore (horns), and Stefan Lessard (bass). There's also a staunch core of other musicians that regularly contribute to the DMB repertoire, most notably the virtuoso guitarist-vocalist Tim Reynolds.

The usual process through which DMB creates music is highly collaborative, dynamic, and often piecemeal. Dave might come up with a guitar groove and some lyrics. Carter finds and defines the groove's rhythm, giving it the appropriate pump. Boyd tears into its melodic bone structure, providing searing new heights and harmonies. Sometimes the roots of a new song might spring up for a short time, begin to take shape, and then disappear underground again, its seed having to inch around for more water and

---

Dave Matthews pours his soul into his music. The Dave Matthews Band live performances are famous for their energy and connection with the audience.

nutrients. The song will then emerge again a few days—perhaps a few weeks—later, perhaps in a hotel room or even during the sound check for a concert. A typical jam might start out with Dave playing a riff from the song, singing some lyrics. Then another member of the band will chime in, and then another, until suddenly the fledgling song's missing elements will emerge and entwine in an act of collaborative magic.

But not this time. Now the guys were stuck, and they were already three months behind schedule in coming up with the songs comprising *Everyday*, the follow-up album to the hugely popular and Grammy-nominated *Before These Crowded Streets*. Dave was seriously down.

But how could Dave Matthews possibly be depressed? Since the formation of DMB in the winter of 1991, the band had virtually climbed the mountain from the club and college town scene to the peak of rock 'n' roll stardom. It had cut two independent albums (*Remember Two Things* and *Recently*) and three studio albums for BMG/RCA Records (*Under the Table and Dreaming*, *Crash*, and *Before These Crowded Streets*). In November of 1999 DMB would issue its independent live CD, *Listener Supported*. The band had been nominated for eight Grammy awards and won one (for Best Rock Performance; "So Much To Say") and had sold well over 15 million CDs. It had performed at President Bill Clinton's 1996 inauguration gala (other guest musicians included Stevie Wonder, Kenneth "Babyface" Edmunds, Trisha Yearwood, James Taylor, Kenny Rogers, and Yo-Yo Ma). In 1998's final tally for concert touring receipts, DMB came in at number two. The band had grossed $40.1 million dollars, trailing only the legendary Elton John at $46.2 million. The June 1998 cover of

Spin magazine proclaimed, "Dave Matthews Is the King of Rock and Roll (Who Knew?)." Dave was by now a millionaire many times over. He had purchased his dream house, a converted flour-mill originally built in 1750, nestled amidst 65 acres in the beautiful foothills of Virginia's Blue Ridge Mountains. So what on earth did Dave have to be depressed about?

There's nothing more important to Dave Matthews than music. Yes, he's a married man now (to Jennifer Ashley Harper) and a new father, too. And yes, he is absolutely devoted to his family and community, both in Charlottesville and Seattle. But the music remains his virtual and artistic heartbeat. It practically flows through his veins, fuels him, as it does all the members of DMB. Drummer Carter Beauford and horn player Leroi Moore grew up on the very same street in Charlottesville. Leroi started off his musical apprenticeship with the alto sax. By high school he had taken up the baritone and tenor saxophone as well. Carter's father, meanwhile, was a jazz trumpeter and an immense influence on his son. Carter's mother said, "As a kid, we knew he had drums in his soul." Violinist Boyd Tinsley also grew up in Charlottesville and had decided he wanted to be a rock 'n' roll star by the time he was in sixth grade. He began his musical studies by mistakenly signing up for what he thought was a guitar class. It turned out to be a course in string orchestra instead, but nevertheless, Boyd never looked back. Last but not least is bass phenomenon Stefan Lessard, the youngest member of the band. Stefan's father has a degree from the Berklee College of Music in Boston. His mother was a recording artist in Spain. Making music is in DMB's blood. Dave says emphatically, "I didn't get into this business to have my face on

MTV or be No. 2 on the charts. All I want to do is play music in front of people. The rest of the stuff can be intoxicating, but it doesn't compare to making music."

Perhaps the roots of Dave and DMB's difficulties in creating their new CD can be traced to their 1997 Grammy Award. The Dave Matthews Band won for "So Much to Say" (*Crash*) as Best Rock Performance. Not quite six years after the band had formed, it had captured one of music's most treasured prizes. But there was a darker, ironic underside to the victory as "So Much to Say" had originally been written in 1992 and was a part of DMB's early club scene and touring repertoire. Now, five years later, the song was being introduced to the world at large as being "new."

DMB was just beginning to drink from one of the age-old realities of the entertainment business—that as hard as it is to get to the top, it's even tougher to stay there. Record producer extraordinaire Steve Lillywhite stated in regards to *Before These Crowded Streets* (Lillywhite had produced this album in addition to the previous *Under the Table and Dreaming* and *Crash*) that "Great bands continually change their boundaries." This premise was in fact going to be the next huge challenge for DMB. Now that the public had become so hungry for its music, how was the band going to strike the balance between creating new, exhilarating tunes and staying true to the "old" sound that its fans expected? In April 1996, DMB had performed on *Saturday Night Live* to help promote *Crash*. Dave remembers having had the opportunity to speak with actor-comedian Jim Carrey. The actor spoke about the sudden changes that celebrity brought into his life. Dave recalls, "He

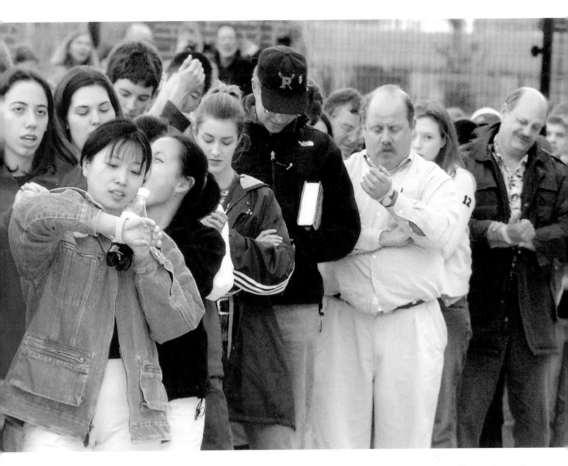

said the strangest part is that you sort of stop being a witness to the people around you . . . you lose the watcher, because you become watched, so that's . . . the most difficult thing." Now, in 1999, how was Dave going to heed Jim Carrey's warning—to avoid the pitfall of being watched? How was he going to instead remain the watcher, the doer, the guy who keeps on making music from his soul regardless of the consequences?

Which brings us back to Charlottesville, 1999 and to the band's basement recording studio. When an RCA record executive flew in from Los Angeles to listen to DMB's new tracks, Dave and the band's worst fears were confirmed. The new

Fans line up for a chance to get early tickets to a Dave Matthews Band concert in Charlottesville, VA. The band's popularity has slowly and steadily increased over the course of their career, and today they are a top concert draw.

material was dark, brooding, downbeat. It was meeting no one's—including the band's own— expectations. Dave later explained, "I don't want to be someone who writes about how sad I am. I'd rather write about these same topics, but with a little momentum. With some sort of strength. Otherwise, I don't think there's any gift—or offering—being made. I would like to be an inspiring force. I want the music to make people think, but not think, 'What's the point?' I was choking. Every song was about dying. Not about living regardless of the fact we're going to die."

A radical change was called for. DMB decided to part ways with producer Lillywhite. Dave flew to L.A. to meet with legendary hit composer- producer Glen Ballard. Subsequent to the meeting, Dave and Glen agreed that Ballard would commandeer DMB's eagerly-awaited new album.

Dave and Glen began working together on the song "Everyday" (the track was based on Dave's original composition, "#36"). The Matthews- Ballard team then proceeded to write nine new songs in 10 days—a veritable creative firestorm! Dave's dry spell had disintegrated as his depression lifted. He recalls, "I felt as though my self-imposed weight of the world, my burden, had been taken off. I started feeling powerful again, feeling the power that we all have. The nearly squashed flame was eagerly burning again."

The result of Dave, Ballard, and DMB's new collaboration was the 12 musical tracks of *Everyday*. The album was released on March 12, 2001 and entered the *Billboard* album chart at number one. It sold 732,000 copies its first week and has currently shipped about four million units. And whereas many loyal fans were disappointed at DMB's scrapping of the original Virginia recording sessions, Dave and the band had made an important, powerful statement. DMB was going to continue making music its own way, on its own terms. It was going to keep its passion bursting from the ashes with gorgeous, haunting melodies and unstoppable energy. And perhaps most of all, it would fight to keep the balance between its unquenchable love of music and the intense commercial pressures that had broken many lesser bands apart. As Dave himself writes in the song, "If I Had It All" from *Everyday*:

> If I were a king
> If I had everything . . .
> If I were giant-sized
> On top of it all
> Then tell me,
> What in the world
> would I sing for?

2

GROWING UP
WITH MUSIC

David John Matthews was born in South Africa on January 9, 1967 and grew up in a suburb of Johannesburg. His father, John, was a respected physicist. His mother, Val, is a painter and a former architect. She's also a fan of classical music, and Dave remembers the sounds of Tchaikovsky, Bach, Beethoven, and Stravinisky wafting through the house in his early years. A grandfather introduced him to Glen Gould's famous recording of Bach's "Goldberg Variations." Growing up, Bach was like pop music to him. Dave recounts, "Although there were no musicians in my family, there was always music playing in the house. And there was the appreciation of long hikes through the woods and family quiet time, where we could listen to the sounds of things around us, heartbeats and footsteps."

It wasn't long before the young David was on the move. You might say that touring was in his blood. His father began working for IBM in New York, and the family settled in the Manhattan suburb of Yorktown Heights when David was two. America, of course, introduced Dave's ear to a specific framework of musical references.

Dave Matthews' earliest home was in Johannesburg, South Africa. The native music in South Africa was one of the influences upon his own musical development.

He remembers hearing the Jackson Five, and it wasn't long before he began listening to Bob Dylan.

In 1974, when Dave was seven, the Matthews family moved again, this time to Cambridge, England. Dave's new musical heroes became the Beatles. He says, "I was very young . . . and I couldn't understand how anybody could make such perfect things." Despite the influence of the Beatles, though, he also became interested in different and diverse strains of rock, including punk rock bands such as the Sex Pistols.

A year later the Matthews clan was back in Yorktown Heights, New York. John Matthews's work as a physicist was beginning to earn him an international reputation. Dave calls him "one of the granddaddies of the superconductor." Back in the United States, Dave was about to face two critical passages. The first at the age of nine, was when he had his first guitar lessons. It was hardly a successful undertaking, and Dave admits, "I was a terrible student." He did manage to learn a few of the simpler Beatles songs. The second occurrence was the tragic death of John Matthews to lung cancer in 1977 when Dave was only ten years old. The Matthews family believes that John's illness was possibly linked to his exposure to radioactive material while working for IBM. The devastating loss spun the family around. Val decided to bring David, his two sisters Ann and Jane, and his brother Peter back to South Africa. Dave remembers that "It was for family that we went back there . . . a single mom with four kids, she wanted to get some support."

Back in Johannesburg while mourning his

father and missing his friends in America, Dave entered the difficult passage from adolescence to adulthood. He attended a British-style private school, but his primary interests veered toward the extra-curricular: fooling around on the guitar, sketching, and listening to music—but not just listening to the music, but really studying it. His younger sister Jane (whom Dave calls his soul mate; one of his first original compositions, co-written with Mark Roebuck, is not coincidentally entitled "The Song That Jane Likes") recalls, "He listened very purposefully. He knew every word to every single Beatles album."

Dave also developed a new, intermittent social circuit. He remembers: "[We] would go out and sit out in the field, go out in the bush and hang out with some guys who worked at my uncle's dairy who were mostly black . . . stay up late and tell stories." Dave's friendship with the black and colored (an important distinction in South Africa's racist apartheid regime) workers also led to new musical explorations. He began to absorb the glorious, complex, and triumphant sounds of artists such as King Sunny Ade, Salif Keita, and Hugh Masekela. Without consciously knowing it, their rhythms began to sink into Dave's musical bone structure. He also developed an affinity for the unique, spellbinding sound of the African drum. Dave's love of percussion helped influence his own choice of instruments. He observes, "Electric guitar is not as much a percussive instrument as an acoustic is. I feel at home with an acoustic because it's hollow; it's got a drum quality."

Inevitably, Dave's journey into South African

music also became a looking-glass into its political and social consciousness. In black and colored South Africa, there was no way to separate the actions of creating and performing music from the brutal reality of institutionalized racism. Dave witnessed people singing "the most incredible music in the face of police with tear gas and bats." He also began to participate in protest marches to end apartheid. And he gradually had to come face-to-face with his mounting frustration with and helplessness at the violence targeted at South African blacks—especially after having spent so much of his youth in the comparatively safe lap of the United States. Dave came to realize that his mother country's state of violence was not only poisonous but constant. It infected the day-to-day health of his immediate world whether it made the daily international headlines or not.

Dave's mother was active in the anti-apartheid movement. The Matthews family was Quaker, and the roots of Val's activism were very much a part of the Quaker tenet of combating social injustice. Dave and his siblings were raised on the precept that prejudice and racism are simply abhorrent and unacceptable. Dave remembers, "We were brought up very, very aggressively, that bigotry and racism are *evil* things, and they stem from fear." It isn't difficult to see how this moral foundation became woven into Dave's music. One of his early DMB songs, "Cry Freedom," was in response to the political and social turmoil in his homeland. First performed in 1991, the song echoes the cry of slain anti-apartheid leader Stephen Biko, who was beaten into a coma by the South African security forces in 1977. The song's lyrics cut to the quick:

> Cry Freedom, cry from deep inside
> Where we all are confined
> While we wave our hands in fire . . .
> How can I turn away?

As a teenager, Dave was already contemplating the arena of social activism that was embodied by some of the great folk musicians and rock and rollers: artists like Woody Guthrie, Bob Dylan, Crosby Stills Nash & Young, Bruce Springsteen, and U2. Certainly, music can be fun and mindless, but it also has the ability to serve a higher purpose—to address social and political ills, and to call for change. From 1982 until 1986, Dave played the guitar constantly. "That's all I did," he recounted in an interview. His vocal style also began to take shape as he fell under the influence of Marvin Gaye and especially Bob Marley, who was a powerful model. It was perhaps no accident that this musician was a powerful voice for social justice in his home country of Jamaica. "He was on the edge, at least socially. And I loved the rhythm," says Dave.

In 1986, Dave was confronted with a fateful decision. He had reached the age of the mandatory military draft in South Africa. If Dave were to reside there, his only choice was to enter the army. He opted to leave the country. Perhaps it was his family's Quaker pacifism that influenced him. Quakers are well-known conscientious objectors to military service as they believe that war causes spiritual damage by inciting hatred. Perhaps it was his distaste for the apartheid government that had crippled so many lives and families. Perhaps it was due to his father's

Dave Matthews and members of the Dave Matthews Band help announce MTV's "Fight for Your Right" scholarships. Growing up in South Africa, Dave fought against apartheid. He has been very socially aware since childhood and the band is active in participating in charitable and social causes.

previous work in the United States, which had helped award Dave official U.S. citizenship. Regardless, Dave emigrated at the age of 19. He not only had the heartfelt spiritual support of Val and his siblings, he had their physical support as well. Before the end of the year, the entire Matthews clan had uprooted itself and moved back across the ocean to America.

CHARLOTTESVILLE

D ave's first stop as an official citizen in the United States was New York City. He landed a temporary job at IBM (where his father John had worked), but soon became disgruntled. His next stop—Charlottesville, Virginia—would have a far deeper impact.

John Matthews had worked at the University of Virginia in Charlottesville long before David was born. The beautiful and well-cultured town had left a powerful imprint upon Val, and she decided to resettle her family there after leaving South Africa in 1986. Dave joined her after his brief stint in New York.

Charlottesville is a town of 50,000 people situated 100 miles southwest of Washington, DC and 70 miles northwest of Richmond, Virginia. It's a unique intersection of college intellectualism and bohemian energy. The surrounding landscape is home to both some of America's premiere horse ranches and artistic innovators. Playwright and actor Sam Shepard, actress Jessica Lange, and novelist Mark Helprin are among those who have staked a claim to this beautiful countryside. One musician in recalling Charlottesville said that it reminded him of the stories he had heard about Paris

Dave Matthews started putting together his band while living in Charlottesville, a city with a rich and vibrant musical community that was full of talented musicians.

in the 1920s. There was a cultural and artistic blossoming at work—a community of painters, actors, writers, poets, and musicians had taken root in a locale that had access to all the resources of the neighboring university. As far as Dave was concerned, Charlottesville became the crossroads of the world—his New York City, his England, and his South Africa all rolled up into one. He studied part-time at a local community college, where he became interested in philosophy, art, and theater. In 1987, after working several temp jobs and basically "wandering" his way around Charlottesville, he got a bartending job at a well-known local watering hole named Miller's.

If Charlottesville was the crossroads of Dave Matthews' new world, then Miller's was the musical crossroads of Charlottesville. Music—the love of it, and the need to create and communicate it—forges its own powerful, magical web of transport. It also creates its own unique network. Miller's was where the best of Charlottesville's local musicians and visiting bands performed, and its small stage and pub essentially became the meeting hub for the Dave Matthews Band-to-be. Dave met guitarist-vocalist Tim Reynolds there. He met Ross Hoffman, who would soon become his good friend and motivator. He met Carter Beauford and Leroi Moore. He met trumpeter John D'earth, who later toured with pianist Bruce Hornsby and also taught music at the Tandem School, where prodigy Stefan Lessard happened to studying. If Dave had spent his first months in Charlottesville "wandering," he had finally wandered into exactly the right place.

Dave first introduced himself to Tim Reynolds at Miller's in 1987. Reynolds was playing with his own band, TR3, and Dave would eventually sit in with them on several occasions. In the meantime, Dave and Tim began experimenting with "little four-track recordings" in the Matthews family basement. In 1990, Dave became close friends with Ross Hoffman, a Miller's regular. Hoffman was also a songwriter and had at one time owned a local recording studio. Dave comments, "Before [1990], I had only doodled around on the guitar and never finished a song, until Ross Hoffman encouraged me, steered me towards writing." Dave started hanging around Ross' apartment building, which has since become famous as "the South Street Warehouse." The friendly, creative energy of the building became immortalized in Dave's 1991 song:

> Maybe things won't be better than
> they have been
> Here in the warehouse
> At the warehouse
> How I love to stay here.

Many of Dave's South African friends had long known about his guitar playing. In America, however, Dave was more secretive regarding his musical passion. Only a select few knew how serious he was about his musicianship. Then— suddenly, it seemed—Dave decided to let the Charlottesville contingent know that he had been writing his own material. "It's weird," he muses. "After a trip to South Africa, I cut off all my hair. Somehow that gave me the confidence to show people my stuff." Dave also realized that to be taken seriously, he needed to lay his material down on tape. He had already done some work with Tim Reynolds and recorded his first demo in November 1990. But he also knew that for his music to reach its fullest potential, he would have to expand his immediate circle.

By early 1991, Dave quit his bartending job bar at Miller's and dedicated himself to challenging and improving his songwriting. Hunkered down in his mother's basement, he would spend every evening from 7 to 11 P.M. writing, rewriting, and progressing. His diligence was further aided by Ross Hoffman's input and critiques. At first, Dave only had four original songs. But he felt the material was strong enough to cut a second demo, and proceeded to seek the help of Carter Beauford and Leroi Moore. Carter was a Charlottesville native whose musical talents were first nurtured by his father, a jazz trumpet player. Carter had actually played his first gig when he was only nine years old. He went on to perform in a multitude of different bands, offering everything from jazz to fusion to disco. Oftentimes Carter played with neighborhood pal Leroi. Leroi had started playing the alto saxophone in junior high school. Along the way he also learned the bass sax, the tenor sax, the flute, and the clarinet. (Today when Leroi tours with DMB, he brings 10 different instruments along with him, switching horns for nearly every song.) Dave had first met Leroi when he was playing a jazz gig at Miller's, and soon Leroi agreed to help him out as well.

Next up was Stefan Lessard. In early 1991, Stefan was only 16 years old. Born in southern California, Stefan and his rather unconventional family had originally arrived in Virginia in 1984 to live in Yogaville, an ashram established by Swami Satchidananda. The Lessards then jumped to Madison, Wisconsin for two years before relocating back to Charlottesville. Stefan was in his junior year at the progressive Tandem School when teacher and musical guru John D'earth introduced him to Matthews. The young

Leroi Moore was another Charlottesville resident who Dave asked to play on a demo tape. Leroi was also friends with Carter Beauford since childhood.

Stefan's impact on the new quartet was immediate. Carter said, "When I first met Fonz he was like fifteen or sixteen and playing upright bass better than a lot of older cats I know who'd been playing longer than he's been alive."

Dave had first heard violinist Boyd Tinsley perform at a college fraternity party. Boyd had grown up in the same Charlottesville neighborhood as Carter and Leroi. He was already playing in two other bands when Dave invited him to lay down tracks for the 1991 demo. Boyd had developed a unique, robust improvisational style that was fueled by a brainstorm he'd had while attending the University of Virginia which pondered, "Why can't a violinist be the lead musician of a rock band?"

The original trio of Dave, Carter, and Leroi suffered through a less-than-promising beginning. Dave said, "The first time we played together . . . we were awful. Not just kind of bad, I mean heinously bad. We tried a couple of different songs and they were all terrible . . . Sometimes it amazes me we even had a second rehearsal." The musicians tried their way with Dave's four existing songs, but there was no concrete sense of sound, arrangement, or direction. Things finally started to click when Stefan joined them. And then came the idea to use Boyd and his violin for the song, "Tripping Billies." A magical connection was starting to take form. By the fledgling band's fourth rehearsal, the group began to think beyond the demo itself, and to conjure the possibility of continuing on afterward as a live band.

The group's first official gig was in April 1991 at an Earth Day celebration. Two hundred people showed up for the event. Dave and the boys were the very last band on the playlist, and as evening set in and the weather grew chilly, only the stragglers remained to listen to a mixed-race quintet that basically no one knew anything about. But by the end of the performance, everyone in the crowd was invigorated and dancing.

Venue by venue, the five musicians set off on the rugged road to musical survival, if not success. One of the things they needed was a name. For one of their first shows, Leroi told a club manager simply to put down "Dave Matthews" on a poster, and a group would definitely show that night. On his own accord, the manager went ahead and wrote "band" after Dave's name. Of course, the fact that Dave had now automatically become the focal point of the group's live appearances is something he still takes with a huge grain of salt. "In fact," he comments, "We should change our name to The Band That Used To Be Called the Dave Matthews Band But Isn't Anymore Because It Was Wrongly Named To Begin With."

Little did any of the band members imagine that not only would the hastily-conceived name stick, but that the "Dave Matthews Band" would become one of the most successful bands of the 1990s.

4

"DAVESPEAK"

A small bar named Eastern Standard on the Downtown Mall in Charlottesville gave DMB its first regular gig. The band played on Tuesday nights, sometimes in front of audiences of two dozen people or less. Many of the musicians playing at Eastern Standard were hoping to one day make the jump one block uptown to the more acclaimed Miller's, where Dave used to tend bar.

As the summer of 1991 passed into the early months of 1992, DMB's focus and direction began to congeal. One of the great frustrations, of course, was that the band wasn't entirely free to pursue its music. The small gigs DMB scored brought in minimal cash, not even close to the amount its members needed to live on. There were families and children to take care of. As a result, the group had to work day jobs rather than go on tour. Additionally, Stefan Lessard's schedule was compromised by his high school obligations. And Boyd Tinsley was committed to his own group, the Boyd Tinsley Band (it wasn't until mid-1992 that he became a full-time member of DMB). In the midst of the band's struggle to carve out a musical toehold, Dave entered an immensely

In concert, Dave Matthews became famous for his stream-of-consciousness banter between songs, known to fans as "Davespeak." Dave opens his mouth and says whatever is in his heart and on his mind on topics ranging from his boxer shorts to favorite television programs.

creative phase as a songwriter. By February 1992 the band's original repertoire had grown from four to fifteen songs, many of which would surface on DMB's first three albums. The tunes "Satellite," "Ants Marching," "What Would You Say," and "Tripping Billies" all emerged from this golden period, as well as the concert anthem "Dancing Nancies." Not bad for a band that a year earlier had come close to dissolving after its first disastrous rehearsal.

In September 1991, the Dave Matthews Band was scheduled to play its first out-of-state engagement—a two-night stand in Colorado. The group, along with its manager, a "roadie," and two friends, in addition to instruments and equipment, jammed into a truck and a car and headed west. Unfortunately, rock and roll glory wasn't exactly waiting in the shadow of the Rocky Mountains. The Road House club, the brand-new venue that had booked them, was already on the verge of bankruptcy. It didn't have the money to advertise and its sound system was poor. DMB was paid $1,000, but the crowd was meager. As soon as DMB left Colorado, the Road House was shut down.

Back in Charlottesville, however, the band's popularity continued to surge. By October 1991, DMB had introduced "Ants Marching" (the song was originally entitled "No New Directions") to its repertoire and was invited to play at a larger, more popular club named Trax. In the years to come, DMB's weekly gigs there would become legendary. In the meantime, the band was introduced to its soon-to-be manager, Coran Capshaw. He owned Trax as well as another club in Richmond, Virginia. He was a fervent Grateful Dead fan and had accrued experience managing a few other rock bands.

Capshaw's deepening involvement with DMB became an important factor in ushering the group toward success and stardom.

Tim Reynolds was another powerful influence on Dave and the band. The virtuoso Charlottesville guitarist played on DMB's first four studio albums, the first live double album, and the EP. Beginning in 1992, Tim and Dave also began a tradition of touring together annually as an acoustic duo. Matthews has commonly referred to Tim as his guitar hero. He says, "The first time I ever got my heart broken by someone who can play so . . . awesomely, it was Timmy."

In 1992 the DMB tide began to rise, and quickly. The band was attracting a large and enthusiastic fanbase in its hometown. The *C-Ville Weekly* ran a cover story on the group in February and asked somewhat prophetically, "Is the Dave Matthews Band the next big thing?" A number of different factors combined to fuel DMB's ascent: the extraordinary talent and creative synchronicity of its members, its charismatic and passionate performances, its unique, stirring songs, and the ever-growing word of mouth surrounding the band's appearances. But perhaps one of the most important elements of its burgeoning popularity was the band's open taping policy.

DMB made a bold and interesting decision early on. The group decided to allow fans to plug their tape decks directly into their soundboard at gigs. Those live, "approved" bootlegs would prove to be an extraordinary boon to DMB as concertgoers proceeded to copy and distribute these tapes across the country at their own expense. People would show up early at shows "to get a spot on the board." During the band's first year, it was possible to get that spot. Afterwards, success made the soundboard awfully crowded. As DMB expanded its touring sched-ule, the taping circuit played an increasingly important role in promoting and marketing the band. Boyd said, "People knew about us [before we toured there]. We'd never been to Alabama before. We'd go to this place, and cars would be lined up down the road, and there'd be all these people going to this big club. We'd be sitting in our red van saying, 'Oh, my God!'" If its fans knew that the DMB was coming, so did the fans' parents. As its popularity grew, DMB actually began receiving letters from parents asking Dave to make sure to send their teenagers home safely from concerts and taper runs!

It's important to differentiate between tape-trading and bootlegging. Tape-trading was pioneered by the Grateful Dead. The group had a motto—"We're not in the record business, we're in the music business." No money changes hands in tape-trading. The dubs are often of inferior quality, and they are passed along to fans and devotees in a heartfelt effort to share and compare the essence of a band's sound, development, and performances. The bootleg business, however, is strictly profit-driven. Its copies are mass-marketed and over-priced, sometimes to the tune of $60 per release. Today, bands such as Phish and Blues Traveler as well as DMB are taper-friendly. Tape-trading is especially relevant to groups like the Grateful Dead and DMB, as these groups' spontaneous, improvisational styles are critical to the fiber of their music. Many early DMB fans could study the band week in and week out. They might hear a song time after time and observe how each rendition might differ, perhaps with the addition of a new verse, a new introduction, a newly-inspired arrangement or jam. Such an

interaction led to a unique bond between DMB and its listeners.

As DMB's popularity grew, so did the need to expand its set list. For a few weeks in the spring of 1992 Dave disappeared with Ross Hoffman. When he returned, he came back with eight new compositions. The band also began to spread its tendrils to other spots on the east coast. Coran Capshaw had them play in Washington, DC, New York, and Philadelphia. DMB was the opening act for bands like Blues Traveler, the BoDeans, and the Connells. They also played at alternative venues such as fraternities and even a debutante party in Lawrenceville, Georgia. For its solo concerts, DMB would jam for up to three hours.

Another unique, fun, and utterly spontaneous happenstance was beginning to emerge as DMB toured. It was a cultural phenomenon that became known as "Davespeak." While onstage, Dave would suddenly and unpredictably start

Violinist Boyd Tinsley signed on with the Dave Matthews Band as a part-time member at first, recording on Dave's demo. But his lead violin proved to be a valuable asset that soon became integral to DMB's unique sound.

talking about whatever came into his mind. The subject matter could be his boxer shorts, or how the *Tonight Show* was his favorite television program. People would talk to Dave onstage between songs and he would talk back. His comic, improvisational quotes became an important part of the performances themselves. The popularity of Davespeak affected a generation of music lovers and DMB fans. Even today, devotees patch into the Internet to keep up with the latest Davespeak gems.

By the end of 1992, DMB had built a repertoire of nearly 30 original songs. For their weekly gig in Charlottesville, the set list included "Granny," "Cry Freedom," "The Song That Jane Likes," "Satellite" (first performed in 1991 under the title "After Her"), "Two Step," "True Reflections," and "One Sweet World." With their songwriting and performing growing stronger by the day, Coran and the band were intent on winning the interest of a major record label. But their attitude was also reminiscent of the baseball film, "Field of Dreams"—"Build it, and they will come," the band seemed to be saying. DMB was planning to produce its own album with or without major sponsorship. On November 9, 1993, the band released the independent *Remember Two Things*. By March 1997 (well after the release of their albums *Under the Table and Dreaming* and *Crash*), *Remember Two Things* went gold, having sold 500,000 units. The success of *Remember Two Things* is nearly unheard of; most independent albums are considered smash hits if they sell 200,000 copies.

On November 1, 1993, DMB signed a recording contract with RCA/BMG records. Ironically, the record deal didn't originate with the impending release of the independent album, but rather with the taper culture. As DMB barnstormed its way up and down the east coast, an intern at RCA Records brought a DMB tape to an executive in Los Angeles. The executive liked what he heard and immediately phoned his New York counter-part. It turned out that the New York executive, Peter Robinson, was actually going to see DMB in concert at the Wetlands that very same night.

Approximately two years and eight months after the members of the Dave Matthews Band laid down tracks for Dave's demo tape, the group had scored a contract with a major industry label. Could success be within reach?

5

CRASH

O n January 9, 1994, Dave Matthews and Tim Reynolds were scheduled to go onstage for an acoustic show at the Wetlands in New York City. Dave addressed the audience, telling them that he had just stepped off the plane that very morning from a 17-hour flight from Johannesburg, South Africa. Dave continued, "That's a country full of lots of violence and lots of hatred. But it's also full of lots of love and lots of good people. But I was there mourning the very recent murder of my sister. So this evening goes out to her and in her memory."

Dave's older sister, Ann, and her husband had been killed in a senseless shooting. For the sake of Ann's children, whom he and Jane Matthews subsequently decided to raise in Virginia, Dave requested that the details of the tragedy not be published.

Often times when looking at the lives of star performers—whether they be in the realm of music, theater, or film—it's easy to focus upon the more obvious, accessible rungs of the artist's rise to success. It's a lot more difficult, however, to examine the invisible underpinnings of his or her drive—to understand the how's, where's, and why's of the creative

The members of the Dave Matthews Band, pictured here with other artists supporting MTV's "Fight for Your Right" campaign, use life experiences to generate music. Often they try to speak from the heart.

process. Dave's music is often infused with uplifting, romantic grooves and stirring melodic transitions. But the beautiful fiber of the music often serves to shield the listener from a song's darker, lyrical roots. Many of Dave's compositions are in fact concerned with the specter and inevitability of death. Long before Ann's demise, of course, there had been the premature passing of Dave's father to deal with. There had also been the death of Miguel Valdez in 1993 from hepatitis. Valdez was an extraordinary percussionist who had occasionally played with the band and had an immense influence on Carter Beauford and former DMB keyboardist Peter Griesar.

In the words to "Seek Up" we hear, "Soon we will all find our lives swept away." In "Lie in Our Graves," Dave sings, "I can't believe that we would lie in our graves/Dreaming of things that we might have been." Death looms even in the DMB anthem "Ants Marching," as the lyrics proclaim "Lights down, you up and die." The tension between dark and light or hope and devastation that resonate throughout much of Dave and DMB's music is a reflection of the author's own life journey. Dave says, "Music will always be a source of healing. It is really like therapy for me. Death is dark and leaves great big holes, but it's also a wonderful way to remind us just how abbreviated life can be and how we should count our blessings."

In a time of great sadness, RCA/BMG Records' involvement with the band offered an important nod to the future. DMB's first major album was on the drawing board, and the group needed a producer. Its choice was Steve Lillywhite, a legendary British musical force. Although Lillywhite wasn't even 40 years old, his roster of clients read like a who's who of modern rock and roll. It included the Rolling Stones, U2, Peter

Gabriel, Aretha Franklin, the Talking Heads, David Byrne, the Psychedelic Furs, Joan Armatrading, and Marshall Crenshaw. Lillywhite was a consummate producer and a perfect match for DMB. His comprehensive technical knowledge was wed to a wonderful eye and ear for the unique blend of voice, songwriting, and instrumentation that constitutes an important band. Lillywhite made a dual promise to DMB, a promise that he was destined to keep. First, he said he wasn't going to change the band's sound. Second, he guaranteed that the upcoming album would go platinum.

As the winter of 1994 intensified, so did DMB's schedule. The band continued to tour from February to April, performing 20 to 25 gigs a month in states spanning from North Carolina to Mississippi to Kansas. Additionally, Dave shouldered most of the burden to write several new songs for the upcoming Lillywhite production (inaugural tour additions were "Get in Line" and "Let You Down," the latter co-written with Stefan Lessard). The hectic schedule and the pressure to perform were particularly difficult for Dave, who was still reeling from Ann's death. In April 1994, DMB released *Recently*, a five-song compilation CD (not under the RCA label) that included live versions of Dave and Tim Reynolds performing "Warehouse" and "Dancing Nancies." Then in May, the band traveled north to Woodstock, New York, with Lillywhite. For the next two months, DMB would work with Lillywhite at Bearsville Studios to create *Under the Table and Dreaming*.

The title of *Under the Table and Dreaming* is a phrase taken from the song "Ants Marching." The concept is rooted in Dave's childhood when he would play under the table and dream about

Stefan Lessard is the youngest member of the Dave Matthews Band and immediately impressed the others with his skill on the bass.

the world of grown-ups. The album sold 30,000 units during its first week of release (September 26, 1994) and debuted on the *Billboard* album chart at number 34—a wonderfully ironic echo to one of the CD's own songs titled "#34." For a debut album to even enter the Top 100 is an extraordinary occurrence, but to be in the Top 40 is phenomenal. Dave dedicated *Under the Table and Dreaming* to Ann Matthews's memory.

One of the reasons for DMB's near-immediate success was the band's ability to reach beyond demographics; to attract listeners of diverse ages and devotees of many different types of music. This ability reflects Dave's own well-traveled background, and particularly his relationship to South Africa and its music. He says of the music's appeal, "I guess the one thing I learned from the music there was that it doesn't have to be aimed at a specific person, it doesn't have to appeal to a 13 year old or a 25 year old or someone who's fifty. Why can't it be aimed at them all?"

One might argue that DMB's musical style is nearly indefinable. It integrates strains of jazz, fusion, funk, rock, and South African folk music. At times the melodies are light and transcendent, like a dream-like mist—while other times they're a percussive engine. The unique, often improvisational contributions of Carter, Leroi, Stefan, and Boyd often make the music's tricky time signatures hypnotizing instead of distracting. A 1995 reviewer from *Daily Variety* nicely encapsulated DMB's sound: "The bulk of the Matthews Band's material starts in riffs and bluesy motifs until the melody is resolved in the sweetest pop chords this side of Sting."

Another interesting aspect to DMB's rise is that it was truly a grassroots phenomenon. In the age of MTV and massive broadband exposure, DMB had made only one music video ("What Would You Say" was filmed in Boulder, Colorado, and started airing in December 1994). The band's ascent was due to a combination of "old-fashioned" qualities: its sound, its energy, its commitment, its talent, and its hard work. There was no smoke and mirrors. And, of course, there was also the unyielding passion and support of DMB's fans. The early tape-trading policy had helped create a community of well-educated, fervent listeners who helped turn even more and more people on to the music. In 1995, an Internet digest called "The Nancies" was established. The Nancies' website provided a home address that would both allow DMB fans to e-mail one another and trade fan-recorded concert tapes *and* offer a serious forum to discuss DMB's music.

On February 24, 1995, DMB made its network television premiere, performing "What Would You

Say" on the *Late Show with David Letterman*. In April they performed on *Saturday Night Live*. By May, *Under the Table and Dreaming* had gone platinum (selling one million albums), just as Lillywhite had promised. The band also made its second music video for "Ants Marching." And DMB introduced two powerful new songs, "#40" and "#41." The beautiful, poignant lyrics of "#41" were in fact a metaphor for Dave and the band's own cohesion and meteoric rise:

> I will go in this way
> And find my own way out
> I won't tell you to stay
> But I'm coming to much more
> Me

Yet another momentous occurrence in 1995 was the band's re-entry into the recording studio, this time to create their second RCA/BMG album, *Crash*. It was to be recorded at Bearsville in Woodstock and also at Green Street Recording Studios in New York. Lillywhite was once again the producer, but the album's emphasis would be very different from that of *Under the Table and Dreaming*. Lillywhite encouraged DMB to experiment more in terms of arrangements, lyrics, and instrumentation.

The "experiment" was a huge success. It compelled the band to improvise, to actively engage in group songwriting, and to bring Carter's unique percussive time signatures to the forefront. Dave said of their songwriting, "The one thing I think is true is that we rise to the occasion because Carter can establish the foundations and Stefan can establish these chord foundations that are so solid that you could stick the Empire State Building on top of them."

Sixteen songs were recorded for *Crash*, and twelve made the final cut. The album was released on April 30, 1996. And although it was met with a range of positive and negative reviews, the *Hollywood Reporter* announced that *Crash* debuted in the number two position for weekly sales. By its second week, the album had passed Hootie and the Blowfish to take over the number one spot. By the end of June, *Billboard*'s cumulative tally listed *Crash* as the 10th most popular album in the entire country.

One day prior to *Crash's* auspicious release, however, Dave was nowhere close to the music industry limelight. Instead he was teaching poetry and music to third graders at a Charlottesville elementary school. He played "Ants Marching," "Satellite," and "I'll Back You Up." Dave answered the children's questions and finally put forth a heartfelt piece of advice: "Find something you really love to do, whether it's a fireman, or a scientist, a photographer, a writer."

Carter Beauford is an accomplished percussionist as well as drummer, offering a wide variety of rhythms to the Dave Matthews Band sound.

6

THE VIEW
FROM HERE

The harder the spotlight began to shine on the Dave Matthews Band, the harder the quintet seemed to concentrate on its music. DMB's dreams were big, and it certainly would have been easy to let the growing hype throw the band off course.

Just how big was DMB getting? The band was asked to play at President Bill Clinton's second inauguration gala at the White House in January 1997. In February 1997, DMB won its first Grammy Award (for "So Much to Say" as Best Rock Performance) at Madison Square Garden in New York. Concurrently, the band was nominated for three more Grammy awards for the following year's consideration: "Too Much" was named in Best Rock Song category, *Crash* as Best Rock Album, and "So Much To Say" as Best Rock Performance by a duo or group. After the Clinton inaugural bash, DMB took a break. Dave, however, forged on. He and Tim Reynolds embarked on a national acoustic tour. The duo played a string of three-hour shows in 1,000- to 2,000-seat venues with no backup band. In Los Angeles, Dave and Tim's February 22, 1997 show sold out in four minutes.

Dave Matthews Band members hold Grammy Awards for Best Rock Performance by a Duo or Group in 1997.

As the summer of 1997 turned to fall, DMB's focus began to shift to its third RCA studio album. Lillywhite would again serve as producer. With the success of *Under the Table and Dreaming* and *Crash*, the band definitely felt that the stakes had been raised. Of the hype surrounding new albums, Dave said, "If you sit down and say that you have to go in a new direction, that's like shooting yourself in the foot. I think we just try to make a good album, and we are only trying to please ourselves. I don't know what anyone else wants. I only know what I want. If we sell 100 records, that's fine. I don't make any rules because once you do that, you cut out all the possibilities."

The band started recording *Before These Crowded* Streets in Sausalito, California, in October 1997. DMB finished its work at Electric Lady Studios in Manhattan in early 1998. Unlike their previous CDs, *Before These Crowded Streets* would contain a majority of songs that hadn't been played and road-tested on DMB's concert trail. As a result, the sound and direction of the upcoming album was a huge topic of discussion on the DMB cyber-space network. Another element fueling fan anticipation was Alanis Morissette's participation in the project. Dave and Alanis had first met at Neil Young's Bridge School Benefit in San Francisco in 1997. The pair had kept in touch, and Alanis visited DMB in Sausalito to listen to some of the rough takes. When the band went to Manhattan to finish the album, she flew in to lay down her tracks.

The songs on *Before These Crowded Streets* reflected both the old and the new. The album included snippets of prior DMB compositions and pieces of songs that had weaved their way in

Dave Matthews plays with Neil Young during the 15th Annual Bridge School benefit in October 2001.

and out of concert performances. There were also bold, new, inventive compositions complimented by an array of brilliant backup singers and musicians (including Alanis and, of course, Tim). One element that remained consistent was the communal effort toward songwriting. "Rapunzel" is credited to Matthews, Stefan, and Carter. "Stay (Wasting Time)" belongs to Dave, Stefan, and Leroi, while "Pig" is attributed to all five band members.

Before These Crowded Streets was released in April 1998. The public's response to the material was overwhelming. The new album sold 420,000 units during its first week of release and entered the *Billboard* charts at number one. Additionally, the album was nominated for a

Best Rock Album Grammy. And as DMB hit the concert trail, their star power proved extraordinary. In the 1998 toll for tour receipts, DMB came in at number two, trailing only Elton John (DMB grossed $40.1 million to Sir Elton's $46.2 million).

The new album also voiced a strong line of protest and social consciousness, reinforcing the grain of activism that runs through much of Dave and DMB's work. The Middle Eastern-tinged "The Last Stop" states:

> Fools we are
> If hate's the gate to peace
> This is the last stop.

In "Don't Drink the Water," the first single to be released from the CD, Dave addresses the land lost by the Native American people. On that particular issue, he comments, "I was in some awesome place—Grand Canyon or Red Rocks—and just imagining an entire civilization that, not long ago in the stream of things, was populated by an entirely different group of people, who, not in their wildest dreams, could have imagined what their world would look like 400 years down the road. That it really wouldn't even include them."

DMB's adherence to social consciousness and humanism can't be underestimated. The band's participation in benefit concerts for AIDS, farm relief, and Tibetan freedom is one aspect of that commitment. But the effort also involves the members' utilizing their own money and resources to help improve lives in their home community of Charlottesville. In 1999, DMB donated $50,000 to renovate Charlottesville's Washington Park and $80,000 to a local skateboard park. In February 2000, the band contributed $250,000 to help launch a 13.6-acre park in Albemarle County, Virginia. In addition, Dave has personally donated money to Nelson Mandela and the cause of democracy in South Africa and has helped build a new research wing at the University of Virginia in memory of his father, John.

On a bold and new front, Dave's concern for the future merged with manager Coran's vision in creating the duo's very own music label. The new company's name was "According To Our Records," or ATO Records. The label's product would be distributed by BMG, and its mission was quite simply to discover "talented songwriters, musicians, and performers for whom there is genuine passion and belief. ATO strives to build career artists. As a truly independent label ATO is steadfast in our commitment to maintaining that focus." The company's first artist was the stunning Welsh singer-songwriter, David Gray. He was a huge hit in England and Ireland, but a virtual unknown in North America. ATO decided to begin their collaboration by re-releasing Gray's fourth album, *White Ladder*. Sales of the album soon leapt from 2,000 to 40,000 units a week.

The Dave Matthews Band, meanwhile, kept its eyes zeroed in on the prize—making music. The band had rented a house in Charlottesville, built a recording studio, and began the process of recording their fourth major label album. The goal, according to Boyd, would be to finish up the studio work in mid-June 1999 and go out on tour. Turmoil, however, was brewing.

Dave and the band were unhappy with the progress of their new material. For the first time in its collective existence, the group seemed to be suffering from writer's block.

Additionally, the music seemed to be consummately dark and brooding, a fact that was further impressed on them by a visiting RCA executive. The new working titles of the album—"Busted Stuff," "Grace Is Gone," "Digging a Ditch"—all echoed the mournful undertone of Dave's creative impetus. Dave recalls: "RCA was saying things like, 'Where's that "Tripping Billies?". . . . I knew what they were saying, but it pissed me off no end. Because what I was saying was, 'Don't you think I'd love to be in a frame of mind to write something upbeat?' But I wasn't. I was feeling as if I had run out. And there was nobody around me—as far as I could see—who could help me in any way."

The past was finally catching up with Dave. Despite some of the joy of that summer (Dave married Jennifer Ashley Harper on August 10, 1999) and the irrefutable success of DMB's musical journey, the deaths and ghosts of Dave's history had to be dealt with. His pace over the last 10 years had been so fast and furious; now, it seemed, the old sadness wanted to finally stake its claim.

The answer to Dave and DMB's creative impasse was a painful one. Dave—after hearing out the advice of RCA and Carter—agreed to meet producer Glen Ballard in Los Angeles. Ballard had worked with Aerosmith and Alanis Morissette and was a successful songwriter (Michael Jackson's "Man in the Mirror" and George Strait's "You Look So Good in Love") in his own right. When the meeting went well, Dave decided to sever DMB's ties with producer Steve Lillywhite, the man who had successfully engineered the band's rise to rock 'n' roll stardom. Divorces are never easy, but thankfully, the parting dialogue was somewhat peaceful. States Dave: "I love Steve as a human being and couldn't respect him more as a professional. Without him we wouldn't be where we are. But we needed to be challenged in a different way."

Glen's challenge was to work with Dave on several new DMB compositions as a co-writer. It was also to streamline the arrangements of the songs themselves. Glen said, "If a Dave Matthews song is usually going to take six minutes to get there, my challenge to them was, 'Let's see if we can do it in half the time, and see if we can get as much music in there that's meaningful.'" Glen also encouraged Dave to experiment with a baritone guitar, which is tuned lower than a six-string electric and higher than a bass.

The result of the Glen Ballard-DMB collaboration was the *Everyday* album, which was released on March 12, 2001. *Everyday* entered the *Billboard* album chart at number one, selling 732,000 units its first week. Its arrival followed a 2000 tour in which DMB grossed $68 million, finishing second only to Tina Turner's farewell tour. And whereas many longtime DMB fans were miffed by the cleaner commercial approach of *Everyday* (they preferred the rawer, more emotional cuts of the "Lillywhite tapes"—the pre-Ballard compositions recorded with Lillywhite in Charlottesville that were subsequently released by Napster), there was no denying that Dave had entered a new and inspired creative phase. He had shaken the dark cape of gloom from his back and rediscovered his voice. And that voice—its source and its ultimate expression—is the reason he's here. According to Dave, "There's always going to be an industry machine. But

Dave Matthews plays a baritone guitar during a performance. Glen Ballard, the Dave Matthews Band's producer for *Everyday*, encouraged Dave to experiment with this unique instrument.

MTV and the labels have nothing to do with the fact that music is made. Rock will be here long after those things have retreated and I have laid down for the last time. The only threat is if we start believing that the source of the music is anywhere but inside ourselves."

CHRONOLOGY

1957   Carter Beauford born on November 2

1961   Leroi Moore born on September 7

1964   Boyd Tinsley born on May 16

1967   Dave Matthews born on January 9 in South Africa

1974   Stefan Lessard born on June 4

1977   Dave's father John dies of cancer; the Matthews family relocates to South Africa from Yorktown Heights, New York, where they had been residing

1986   Dave returns to America; revisits New York, then moves to Charlottesville; rest of his family also moves from South Africa to Virginia

1987   Dave begins working at Miller's, a well-known pub and a crossroads for Charlottesville's burgeoning music scene

1991   The newly formed Dave Matthews Band convenes to lay tracks for its first ensemble demo tape; DMB plays its first gig at an Earth Day celebration

1993   DMB releases the independent CD *Remember Two Things*; DMB signs a recording contract with RCA/BMG Records

1994   *Under The Table of Dreaming* released

1995   DMB makes its network television premiere on *The Late Show With David Letterman*

1996   *Crash* released

1998	*Before These Crowded Streets* released; Dave and manager Coran Capshaw form their own music recording label, ATO (According To Our) Records
1999	Dave Matthews marries Jennifer Ashley Harper on August 10
2001	*Everyday* released

ACCOMPLISHMENTS

Discography

1993   *Remember Two Things*

1994   *Recently* (EP)
               Under the Table and Dreaming

1996   *Crash*

1997   *Live at Red Rocks, 8/15/95*

1998   *Before These Crowded Streets*

1999   *Listener Supported*
               Dave Matthews and Tim Reynolds Live at Luther College

2001   *Everyday*
               Dave Matthews Live in Chicago 12.19.98

Awards

1996   Grammy Award for "So Much To Say" – Best Rock
               Performance by a Duo or Group with Vocal

2000   My VH-1 Music Awards – "Coolest Fan Web Site" [Nancies.org]

2001   My VH-1 Music Awards – My Favorite Group
               Must Have Album (*Everyday*)
               Song of the Year ("The Space Between")

FURTHER READING

Delancey, Morgan. *The Dave Matthews Band: Step into the Light.* Toronto: ECW Press, 2001

ABOUT THE AUTHOR

ERIK KEITH ANJOU was born in the Philadelphia area. After graduating from the William Penn Charter School in Germantown, he was fortunate to jump the accelerated train to higher education, having attended Middlebury College (B.A.), Northwestern University (M.A.) and the American Film Institute's Center for Advanced Film Studies (Directing Program). Erik has sustained a foothold across a broad range of filmic and literary pursuits. He has written and directed several feature and documentary films, and most recently has completed his first novel. Erik currently resides in New York City and revisits Philadelphia often to play with his niece, Eliza Sophie, and root on the Flyers.

Photo Credits:

INDEX